"EMILY'S RECIPES ARE PURE DELICIOUSNESS. THEY ARE BEAUTIFUL, NOURISHING AND CRAVE-WORTHY. THIS BOOK IS A MUST FOR ANYONE LOOKING TO GET A CREATIVE TWIST ON QUICK BUT HEALTHY SNACKS AND MEALS."

—AMY LYONS, AUTHOR OF *FRAGRANT VANILLA CAKE*

"FROM HER PHOTOGRAPHY, TO THE PERSONAL TOUCH ON HER WRITING, TO EACH MOUTH-WATERING RECIPE, EMILY SHOULD BE SO PROUD. HER RECIPES HAVE THE WOW FACTOR EVERY TIME AND WOULD GET ANY FOODIE EXCITED ABOUT EATING RAW FOOD."

—RACHAEL CAMPBELL, AUTHOR OF *REVOLUTIONARY RAW RECIPES*

"EMILY'S RECIPES AND PHOTOGRAPHY ARE BEAUTIFUL! SHE MAKES HEALTHY EATING AND COMPASSIONATE LIVING A BREEZE."

—EMMA POTTS, COCONUTANDBERRIES.COM

"WHEN I'M IN NEED OF INSPIRATION, I CRACK OPEN ONE OF EMILY'S RAW COOKBOOKS. HER PAGES ARE ABSOLUTELY FILLED WITH ENTICING, OUT-OF-THE-BOX FOOD IDEAS."

—ERIN IRELAND, ITSTODIEFOR.CA

"EMILY'S BEAUTIFUL RECIPES SHOW HER FLAIR FOR CREATIVITY, HER PASSION FOR NATURAL INGREDIENTS AND HER LOVE OF HARM-FREE LIVING. HONEST, DELICIOUS GOODIES THAT WILL HAVE THE WORLD TURNING VEGAN."

—SOPHIE MACKENZIE, WHOLEHEARTEDEATS.COM

"EMILY'S BOOK IS FULL OF BRILLIANCE AND BEAUTY! THIS IS A MUST-HAVE COLLECTION FOR THOSE WHO CRAVE SIMPLE WHOLESOME FOODS!"

—DAVID AND NOELLE MCGINNIS, AUTHORS OF *SACRED COOKIES AND ELIXIRS*

"EMILY'S GREATEST STRENGTH IS TAKING SIMPLE, NUTRITIOUS INGREDIENTS AND SHOWCASING THEM IN VIBRANT RECIPES THAT ARE ALWAYS DELICIOUS."

-TREVOR ELLESTAD, WRITER, TRAINED YOGA TEACHER AND TRAINED HERBALIST

DEDICATED TO YOU, AS ALWAYS.

PAGE STREET
PUBLISHING CO.

First published in 2014 by
Page Street Publishing Co.
27 Congress Street, Suite 103
Salem, MA 01970
www.pagestreetpublishing.com

Distributed by Macmillan; sales in Canada by The Canadian Manda Group; distribution in Canada by
The Jaguar Book Group.

17   16   15   4   5

ISBN-13: 978-1-62414-091-4
ISBN-10: 1-62414-091-2

Library of Congress Control Number: 2014940718

Cover and book design by Page Street Publishing Co.
Photography by Emily von Euw

Printed and bound in China

Page Street is proud to be a member of 1% for the Planet. Members donate one percent of
their sales to one or more of the over 1,500 environmental and sustainability charities across
the globe who participate in this program.

100 BEST JUICES, SMOOTHIES
AND HEALTHY SNACKS

EASY RECIPES FOR NATURAL ENERGY AND
WEIGHT CONTROL THE HEALTHY WAY

EMILY
VON EUW

AUTHOR OF THE BESTSELLING *RAWSOME VEGAN BAKING*

PAGE STREET
PUBLISHING CO.

CONTENTS

INTRODUCTION

The fact that you have picked up this book and are reading this (willingly, I hope!) means you already have some interest in healthy living and delicious recipes. Phew! Let me just wipe the sweat from my brow. But I understand that this doesn't mean you're a juicing pro or even know what "juicing" really entails. It's all good, though; I've written this book with you in mind. The following pages provide easy-to-understand descriptions and explanations of all things to do with juices, smoothies and healthy snacks, as well as about a hundred kick-ass recipes that everyone can appreciate and *actually* make. If you don't know the first thing about juicing, you will soon. (Then you'll learn the second, and third and fourth...) If you are already pretty savvy with a juicer and blender, I bet I can still teach you a thing or two, or at the very least give you some new recipe ideas. Now back to the shindig.

Okay, hold up the shindig for two seconds. I just wanna say that I highly recommend buying organic. Organic produce supports honest farmers and environmental sustainability and gets you the most delicious fruits and veggies on earth. At the same time, I understand organic is more expensive and not in everyone's budget, and I mean, you're already reading a book about juicing so you're way ahead of where most people are at—high five, buddy. But if you can afford to buy organic, do it. Then you don't have to peel your produce; just give it a rinse to get that dirt off. Back to the shindig.

We need to first ask why anyone should actually care about making and drinking juices and smoothies. I'm not going to turn this into an encyclopedia of nutrition because (1) I am not equipped, (2) all that info exists on the Internet and in other books already and (3) you probably don't want that much detail anyway. But if you are one of those people that want all the nitty gritty deets (that makes two of us), check out my list of recommended resources (page 194), and other info in the back of the book, which I recommend reading first anyway.

JUICE

Let's start with juice. When talking about juice in this book, I am referring to the liquid we can extract from fruits and vegetables. This liquid is full of all the nutrients and vitamins that are in the plants being juiced; the rest is just fiber. When you juice fruits and veggies, you are essentially squeezing all the nutrition out of them (which is found in the juice), leaving behind only fiber. Here's where you might ask, "But isn't fiber good for me?" You're right. A diet high in fiber is a plan for a healthy gut and long life. Having said that, as long as you're already eating a high-fiber diet, adding juices to it is an excellent thing to do. The benefits of juicing are numerous and substantial. Without the fiber to digest, your body can literally absorb the nutrients right away... I mean, in like 15 minutes all that good stuff will be flowing through your blood. When you juice fruits and veggies, your body can absorb more nutrition than if you simply ate the same amount of plants, and you can also consume more. For example, when was the last time you ate a pound of carrots for breakfast? (If you say this morning, you deserve a round of applause because you are officially the carrot champion.) But I'm guessing you'll say never. No one wants to chew that much, and even if you did, your mouth does not have the capability to break down the vitamins and nutrients as well as a juicer. You can easily drink the juice of a pound of carrots and instantly and effortlessly absorb all the benefits just by swallowing. **Note: Don't juice the seeds in fruit, because they contain small amounts of protective toxins. (Probably not enough to be harmful, but I'm a firm believer in "Better safe than sorry.")**

SMOOTHIES

What about smoothies? The difference between smoothies and juice is that with smoothies, you are not taking out the fiber, you're simply blending up fruits and vegetables with water or other liquid until they're smooth and drinkable. Fiber is a necessary part of a healthy diet: it keeps everything moving and it sustains a happy digestive system and that in itself basically keeps the rest of your body happy and humming. The benefits of smoothies are a bit simpler to explain because I'm assuming you already know that eating plants is good for you (I almost typed "pants" there... good thing I caught that because I don't think trousers contain much vitamin C). Getting back on track, smoothies are literally straight-up plants; all you are doing is blending them until smooth. The advantage to this is less work for your digestive system. There's no physical breakdown required because a smoothie is already in the form your stomach wants it: liquid. These drinks make up the bulk of my diet. With smoothies, you're skipping a step and thus getting the nutrients and vitamins in the fruits and veggies absorbed faster. Thumbs up.

CHAPTER 1

SWEET JUICES

Everybody loves fruit juice. It's sweet, fresh as well as refreshing and great for you! So with that logic, I think this will probably be a very popular chapter. You can juice almost any fruit (except for bananas and avocados) into an incredibly delicious elixir of health and glowing color. A lot of my sweet juice recipes also include dark leafy greens and non-sweet fruits (think cucumbers, bell peppers and lemons), not only to balance out the sweetness but also to add extra nutrition. For example, kale is mega-good for your bod and if I can sneak it in with some pineapple, I'm gonna.

Keep in mind that when you juice plants, you're taking out the fiber. Fiber slows down digestion, assimilation and absorption so when you get rid of it, you speed all that stuff up. This is the main benefit to making and drinking juice, but for those of us with sensitive blood sugar levels, it can be an issue because the sugars in the juice are almost instantly absorbed. Personally this is not a problem for me—I can drink a huge glass of pure watermelon juice and be begging for more—but every body is different so I thought it'd be wise to mention this. Fortunately, most of my sweet juice recipes aren't really super sweet anyway, and this is the only chapter you need to be concerned about this with.

Again, as a reminder, do not juice seeds as they can be toxic!

LIME AND APPLE AURA

YOUR BODY WILL LOVE YOU FOR DRINKING THIS, AND IT WILL SHOW BOTH INSIDE AND OUT. APPLES ARE GREAT FOR THE SKIN, AND LIMES ARE TERRIFIC FOR YOUR DIGESTIVE SYSTEM. I THINK THIS RECIPE IS REMINISCENT OF "LIMEADE."

2 green apples
2 limes
1 cucumber

Wash, peel and chop the produce as needed, removing any seeds from the fruit. Put everything through your juicer, sip, get the glow.

LUSCIOUS
LIVER TONIC

ALL THE INGREDIENTS IN THIS JUICE HELP TO INCREASE LIVER FUNCTION AND
KEEP "EVERYTHING MOVING." THIS IS A GREAT DETOX RECIPE, OR THE PERFECT
WAKE-ME-UP IN THE MORNING!

8 radishes
2 green apples
2 beets
4 carrots
1 tbsp (15 g) ginger

Wash, peel and chop the produce as needed, removing any seeds from the fruit. Put everything
through a juicer and enjoy.

SWEET SUNSHINE

GINGER IS AN EXCELLENT BLOOD CLEANSER, AND PINEAPPLE AND LEMON WORK TO
ALKALIZE YOUR STOMACH, CREATING A HAPPY HABITAT FOR DIGESTION (A HEALTHY
GUT = A HEALTHY YOU). FINALLY, BELL PEPPERS CARRY A SURPRISINGLY HIGH AMOUNT
OF VITAMIN C. ALL THE INGREDIENTS COMBINED CREATE A VIBRANT, GLOWING YELLOW
JUICE THAT WILL IMPRESS EVEN THE MOST SKEPTICAL FOLKS.

1 yellow bell pepper
1 tbsp (15 g) ginger
1 lemon
2 cups (330 g) pineapple
3 red apples

Wash, peel and chop the produce as needed, removing any seeds from the fruit. Put through your
juicer and enjoy in the sun!

CITRUS SITUATION

SO. MUCH. CITRUS. HOPEFULLY YOU WERE SPARED FROM THE BRAIN-NUMBING EFFECTS OF A REALITY TV SHOW CALLED *JERSEY SHORE*, BUT SADLY I WAS NOT, AND I THINK MY SUBCONSCIOUS HAD SOMETHING TO DO WITH NAMING THIS ONE. "WE'VE GOT A SITCH!"

3 grapefruits
2 lemons
2 green apples
3 oranges

Wash, peel and chop the produce as needed, removing any seeds from the fruit. Then juuuuuice!

KUMQUATS
BE KIND

WOW! I HAD NEVER HAD KUMQUATS BEFORE MAKING THIS JUICE, AND I WAS BLOWN
AWAY BY THEIR UNIQUE AND FRESH FLAVOR! CITRUSY, SWEET AND SUPER JUICY—THEY
ARE LIKE LITTLE EXPLOSIONS OF SUNSHINE IN YOUR MOUTH. TRY TO BUY THEM
ORGANIC! NOTE: YOU CAN LEAVE THE KUMQUATS WHOLE, NO NEED TO PEEL 'EM.

2 cups (290 g) kumquats
1 orange bell pepper
2 oranges
2 red apples
1 cucumber

Wash, peel and chop the produce as needed, removing any seeds from the fruit. Then throw it all in
the juicer!

KALE AND CARROT KARMA

GOOD VIBES ABOUND! CARROTS ARE FULL OF FEEL-GOOD VITAMINS, AND THEIR COLOR ALONE IS ENOUGH TO CHEER ME UP. KALE IS ONE THE MOST NUTRIENT-DENSE FOODS ON THIS PLANET, AND THE MOST EFFICIENT WAY TO ABSORB THOSE NUTRIENTS IS BY JUICING THE LEAVES. THIS IS A GREAT MORNING JUICE TO WAKE UP YOUR BODY AND MIND! I LOVE SIPPING IT AFTER PRACTICING YOGA.

6 carrots
2 green apples
1 garlic clove
5 cups (335 g) kale
1 cucumber

Wash, peel and chop the produce as needed, removing any seeds from the fruit. Put everything through your juicer, then feel the karma waves.

BUDDHA-FUL BEETS

EARTHLINESS IN ABUNDANCE! I ABSOLUTELY ADORE BEET JUICE. ITS SUBTLE
SWEETNESS AND EARTHY TONES CREATE A WONDERFUL DRINK AND WHEN PAIRED
WITH HERBS (AS IN THIS RECIPE), IT CAN'T BE BEET! WHOOPS—I MEANT BEAT...
NO I DIDN'T.

3 beets
1 cup (16 g) cilantro
1 red apple
1 lime

Wash, peel and chop the produce as needed, removing any seeds from the fruit. Put everything
through your juicer, going slowly with the beets because they're very dense.

SO FRESH, SO CLEAN

THIS IS A SUPER HYDRATING DRINK, FULL OF AMAZINGLY JUICY AND FLAVORFUL INGREDIENTS: CUCUMBER, WATERMELON AND PINEAPPLE. ADD SOME COCONUT WATER AND/OR A PINCH OF SALT (FOR ELECTROLYTES) AND THIS IS THE PERFECT THING TO SIP DURING A WORKOUT! THE FRESH MINT LEAVES ROUND OFF THE DRINK AND MAKE FOR A DELICIOUS, REFRESHING ELIXIR. P.S. THE NAME OF THIS RECIPE IS INSPIRED BY THE *FUNKALICIOUS* OUTKAST TRACK. GIVE IT A LISTEN.

½ watermelon
1 cucumber
2 cups (330 g) pineapple
1 cup (25 g) mint leaves
1 cup (5 g) ice cubes

Wash, peel and chop the produce as needed, removing any seeds from the fruit. Juice the watermelon, cucumber and pineapple. Serve with ice and mint leaves. *Ahhh.*

PEPPERMINT
PICK ME UP

REFRESHING, SWEET AND SURE TO HELP OPEN YOUR EYES IN THE MORNING, THIS JUICE IS ALSO GREAT FOR CALMING AN UPSET TUMMY, THANKS TO THE GINGER AND MINT.

1 cucumber
2 green apples
1 cup (25 g) mint leaves
1 tbsp (15 g) ginger

Wash, peel and chop the produce as needed, removing any seeds from the fruit. Put them all through your juicer and get your morning started right!

HONEY-TO-DEW LIST

MY PARENTS AND I THOUGHT WE WERE SO CLEVER WHEN WE CAME UP WITH THE NAME FOR THIS ONE. GET IT? TO-DO LIST? HONEY-TO-DEW LIST? HONEYDEW MELON? OKAY— CLEVER OR LAME, THIS RECIPE TASTES GREAT. IT'S SUBTLY SWEET, AND THE LIME BRINGS ON A LOT OF FRESH FLAVOR. SIP IT IN THE SUMMER!

1 honeydew melon
2 grapefruits
1 lime

Wash, peel and chop the produce as needed, removing any seeds from the fruit. Then put through your juicer and enjoy!

FENNEL CITRUS SUSTENANCE

THE MYRIAD OF GLIMMERING CITRUS FRUITS AS WELL AS THE FENNEL IN THIS RECIPE ALL COME TOGETHER TO CREATE A JUICE THAT HAS THE PERFECT BALANCE OF SWEET AND TART; IT'S NOW ONE OF MY FAVORITE JUICES. BLOOD ORANGES ARE ONE OF THE MOST GORGEOUS FRUITS I HAVE EVER SEEN!

2 blood oranges
2 cups (175 g) fennel
1 grapefruit
1 lime
2 oranges

Wash, peel and chop the produce as needed, removing any seeds from the fruit. Try to keep some pith on the oranges—it's got lots of nutrients!

SEXY SATISFYING WATERMELON JUICE WITH PEPPERMINT

IF "FOOD PORN" IS A LEGITIMATE TERM, CAN "JUICE PORN" BE A THING, TOO?
I MEAN, LOOK AT THIS PHOTO.

1 watermelon
¼ cup (6 g) peppermint leaves
3 ice cubes

Chop up the watermelon and then blend it into juice—it will liquify almost immediately. I blended up my watermelon in two batches because it was huge. Strain your juice and then pour it over ice and mint leaves. Slurp! So hydrating and sweet!

POWER GREENS

AN ALL-AROUND GREAT GREEN JUICE
RECIPE THAT WILL GIVE YA EVERYTHING
YOU NEED IN ONE GLASS.

4 cups (270 g) kale
1 cup (16 g) cilantro
1 cucumber
1 tbsp (15 g) ginger
1 garlic clove
1 green apple
1 lemon

Wash, peel and chop the produce as needed,
removing any seeds from the fruit. Put through
your juicer and savor the nourishment that
comes out.

EVERYDAY JUICE

THIS IS MY MOM'S GO-TO JUICE EVERY
MORNING AND AN EXCELLENT WAY
TO START YOUR DAY.

1 grapefruit
2 green apples
2 carrots
1 cucumber
1 tbsp (15 g) ginger
1 orange

Wash, peel and chop the produce as needed,
removing any seeds from the fruit. Then put it
all through your juicer and enjoy.

CARROT APPLE LIME

THIS ONE MIGHT MAKE YA PUCKER YOUR LIPS BECAUSE OF THE TARTNESS OF THE LIME—BUT I LOVE IT.

6 carrots
2 red apples
2 limes

Wash, peel and chop the produce as needed, removing any seeds from the fruit. Put it all through the juicer and enjoy!

WATERMELON WAKE ME UP

ONE OF THE MOST REFRESHING AND SEXY DRINKS IN THIS BOOK. NO JOKE.

½ watermelon
1 lime
1 cucumber

Wash, peel and chop the produce as needed, removing any seeds from the fruit. Juice it up!

HERB HAPPINESS

THIS ONE TASTES PRETTY UNUSUAL...BUT I THINK IT TASTES WEIRD IN A GOOD WAY.
I HOPE THAT MAKES SENSE.

1 cup (16 g) mint leaves
1 cup (16 g) cilantro
1 green apple
1 orange

Wash, peel and chop the produce as needed, removing any seeds from the fruit. Juice. Savor the odd flavor.

STRAWBERRY LEMONADE

PERFECT FOR SUMMER. ENJOY A TALL GLASS OF HEALTH AND DELICIOUSNESS
ALL AT ONCE.

2 cups (288 g) strawberries
1 lemon
1 pineapple
½ cup (2.5 g) ice

Wash, peel and chop the produce as needed, removing any seeds from the fruit. Then juice
everything, serve with ice and enjoy.

LETTUCE TURNIP THE BEET

I CAN'T TAKE CREDIT FOR THE PUNNY TITLE. IT'S BEEN GOING AROUND THE INTERNET FOR A WHILE, MAKING PEOPLE FROM ALL WALKS OF LIFE GROAN AT THE LAME HUMOR PLANTS PROVIDE.

2 beets
1 head lettuce
3 turnips
3 carrots
2 green apples

Wash, peel and chop the produce as needed, removing any seeds from the fruit. Juice. Drink!

CHAPTER 2

SAVORY JUICES

Here's the deal: Savory juices are flipping amazing (that was more my opinion than a deal... but shh). Maybe when I say juice, you just think I mean sweet fruit juices. Nope. Vegetables juice wonderfully into flavorful fountains of all colors and potencies. If you're looking to lose weight, these savory veggie juices are your new best friend. I'm talkin' BFFs here. Why is this? Vegetables are extremely low in calories, high in water content and incredibly nutrient dense. That means you can eat—or drink—them to your heart's content and effortlessly find your natural healthy weight. Drink vegetable juice—especially with dark leafy greens— every day for a long life and a beautiful figure.

MEAN, GREEN AND CLEAN

THIS IS A GREAT JUICE TO START YOUR DAY WITH. IT INCLUDES A BUNCH OF WATER-RICH INGREDIENTS AS WELL AS POWERFUL DISEASE FIGHTERS (IF IT'S DARK GREEN AND LEAFY, IT'S PROBABLY AMAZING FOR YOU).

2 cups (135 g) kale
2 green apples
1 lime
3 celery stalks
1 cup (60 g) parsley
1 garlic clove
1 green bell pepper
1 cucumber

Wash, peel and chop the produce as needed, removing any seeds from the fruit. Put everything through your juicer, alternating between greens and juicy fruits to keep the juicer lubricated. Sip up the nutrition with a smile!

V8^2

WHY IS IT SQUARED? BECAUSE THIS RECIPE PACKS TWICE THE NUTRITIONAL PUNCH! I AM AWARE THAT SQUARING SOMETHING DOES NOT REALLY MEAN MULTIPLYING IT BY TWO, BUT LET'S JUST SUSPEND MATHEMATICAL REALITY FOR A SECOND SO WE CAN GET EXCITED ABOUT THIS JUICE; IT'S GOT <u>ALL</u> THE GOOD THINGS.

3 tomatoes

1 lemon

1 garlic clove

1 tbsp (15 g) ginger

1 green apple

1 orange

1 grapefruit

1 cucumber

3 carrots

2 cups (32 g) cilantro

1 cup (16 g) peppermint

2 cups (134 g) kale

1 bell pepper

2 golden beets

3 celery sticks

3 pineapple slices

Wash, peel and chop the produce as needed, removing any seeds from the fruit. Juuuuuuice it all up.

KALE CRAVER

THE FIRST TIME I MADE THIS RECIPE AND TOOK A SIP I IMMEDIATELY EXCLAIMED,
"YOU ARE WHAT I HAVE BEEN CRAVING!" HENCE THE NAME OF THE DRINK. GET
ENERGIZED, NOURISHED AND HYDRATED ALL IN ONE GLORIOUS GLASS. THAT'S
WHAT I'M TALKIN' 'BOUT.

2 green apples
3 cups (201 g) kale
6 celery sticks
1 cucumber
1 garlic clove
1 tbsp (15 g) ginger
1 lemon

Wash, peel and chop the produce as needed, removing any seeds from the fruit. Put everything
through your juicer and drink up the goodness.

TOMATO GARLIC GREATNESS

I WAS GONNA CALL THIS ONE "POWER TO THE PROSTATE" BECAUSE TOMATOES ARE EXCELLENT FOR SAID MALE ORGAN, BUT I DIDN'T WANT TO EXCLUDE US PROSTATE-LACKING LADIES FROM THE SPECIFIC BENEFITS; TOMATOES ARE FULL OF NUTRIENTS THAT ARE BENEFICIAL FOR BOTH SEXES.

2 garlic cloves
5 tomatoes
3 carrots
1 cucumber

Wash, peel and chop the produce as needed. If you're using an organic cucumber, you can leave the skin on! Juice it all. Feel the power.

JICAMA SWEETHEART

THE NAME IS A LITTLE DECEIVING BECAUSE THIS RECIPE ISN'T ACTUALLY ALL THAT SWEET IN FLAVOR OR IN SUBTLETY! THE ONIONS, GARLIC AND GINGER MAKE FOR ONE POWERFUL POTION AND I PROMISE YOU WILL BE FEELING THE DETOXIFICATION AND BLOOD-CLEANSING EFFECTS AS SOON AS YOU START SIPPING THIS. SERIOUSLY, DRINK IT SLOWLY.

4 cups (385 g) jicama
¼ cup (38 g) onion
1 garlic clove
1 tbsp (15 g) ginger
1 lemon
1 green apple (optional)

Wash, peel and chop the produce as needed. Remove the seeds from the apple. Put everything through a juicer. If it's too strong for you, add an apple or two.

VELVET VIBRATIONS

IF YOU LISTEN TO BOOTSY COLLINS, THEN YOU'LL KNOW THIS RECIPE'S NAME IS INSPIRED BY "LOVE VIBRATIONS," OR I GUESS YOU COULD THINK OF THE BETTER KNOWN BEACH BOYS HIT, "GOOD VIBRATIONS." BUT ALSO, WHEN I THINK OF VELVET I THINK OF SMOOTHNESS, AND THE INGREDIENTS IN THIS JUICE ARE ALL EASY ON THE TUMMY AND USEFUL FOR IMPROVED DIGESTION—KEEPING THINGS RUNNING SMOOTHLY. WATCH OUT FOR THE ONION, THOUGH!

4 beets
6 small carrots
1 garlic clove
1 cucumber
1 bell pepper
1 cup (16 g) peppermint leaves
2 tomatoes
¼ cup (38 g) onion
3 small zucchini

Wash, peel and chop the produce as needed, removing any seeds from the fruit, then put through your juicer. This one is really nice strained.

VIRUS VIGILANTE

YOU CAN CALL THIS ONE FLU FIGHTER IF YA WANT, BUT I FEEL LIKE EVERY JUICE BAR HAS A DRINK CALLED THAT, AND I'M TRYING TO BE ORIGINAL. GIMME A BREAK, OKAY? THE IMPORTANT THING IS THAT THIS JUICE IS ONE POTENT TONIC! TOUTING OVER 1200% OF YOUR DAILY REQUIRED VITAMIN C (THANKS TO THE CAMU CAMU POWDER), IT WILL PROBABLY KICK ANY SICKNESS YOU MIGHT FEEL COMING ON. PLUS, IT'S DELICIOUS.

1 lemon
1 garlic clove
1 tbsp (15 g) ginger
1 green apple
1 tbsp (7 g) camu camu powder

Wash, peel and chop the produce as needed, removing any seeds from the fruit, then put it all through your juicer. Throw the juice in a blender with the camu camu powder and blend for just a sec until it is incorporated. Chug!

CARROT GINGER SIPPER

SIP IT SLOW, BECAUSE THE GINGER IS POTENT!

3 carrots
1 tbsp (15 g) ginger
1 red apple
1 lemon

Wash, peel and chop the produce as needed, removing any seeds from the fruit. Put everything through your juicer and enjoy!

LETTUCE AND FENNEL FENG SHUI

THIS RECIPE IS GREAT FOR SETTLING UPSET STOMACHS OR EASING DIGESTION, THANKS TO THE FENNEL. THE OTHER INGREDIENTS ALL HELP WITH BLOOD FLOW AND DETOXIFICATION. CHEERS TO A BALANCED LIFE FULL OF CHI (VITAL UNIVERSAL ENERGY)!

6 cups (330 g) lettuce
1 cucumber
1 lime
1 cup (87.5 g) fennel
1 green apple

Wash, peel and chop the produce as needed, removing any seeds from the fruit. Put it all through the juicer and sip up the good vibes.

SPRING CLEANER

SUPA FRESH! SUPA GOOD! THE PERFECT WAY TO START YOUR MORNING AND KEEP
YOUR BODY HAPPY, HEALTHY, HYDRATED AND GLOWING.

1 green apple
5 cups (650 g) kale
1 lemon
1 cucumber

Wash, peel and chop the produce as needed, removing any seeds from the fruit. Throw through
your juicer and enjoy!

SALSA SEDUCTION

MY FRIEND FROM MEXICO TELLS ME THAT THIS IS BASICALLY PICO DE GALLO, MINUS THE SUPER SPICY SERRANO PEPPER. I CAN DIG IT...I MEAN, DRINK IT!

1 garlic clove
1 cup (180 g) tomatoes
1 cup (16 g) cilantro
1 lime
1 yellow bell pepper
½ cucumber
¼ cup (62 g) onion (optional)
¼ tsp ground cumin

Wash, peel and chop the produce as needed. Remember to remove the seeds from the bell pepper and then put it all through the juicer (except the cumin). Mix the cumin into the juice and enjoy!

RADICAL ROOTZ

ROOT VEGGIES ARE SUPER GREAT FOR YOU BECAUSE THEY TAKE IN ALL THE NUTRIENTS IN THE SOIL THEY ARE GROWING IN, AND THEY HAVE AN AMAZING EARTHY FLAVOR THAT I AM DEEPLY IN LOVE WITH. BESIDES, THE COLOR OF THIS JUICE IS A WORK OF ART IN ITSELF.

3 beets
6 carrots
1 tbsp (15 g) ginger
1 celeriac root

Wash, peel and chop the produce as needed. Throw it all through the juicer and enjoy!

KIDNEY CONSCIOUS

THE MAIN INGREDIENT IN THIS RECIPE IS CELERIAC (OR CELERY ROOT), WHICH IS KNOWN TO PLAY A ROLE IN DETOXIFICATION AND STIMULATING KIDNEY FUNCTION. NOT SURPRISINGLY, THE FLAVOR IS SIMILAR TO CELERY: REFRESHING AND LIGHT. I LIKE TO PAIR IT WITH CITRUS.

1 celeriac root
1 grapefruit

Wash, peel and chop the produce as needed, removing any seeds from the fruit. Juice.

SUNNY SIDE UP

THE SPECIAL INGREDIENT IN THIS RECIPE IS SUNCHOKES (OFTEN CALLED JERUSALEM ARTICHOKES). SIMILAR TO GINGER ROOT IN APPEARANCE, SUNCHOKES HAVE A DELICIOUS FLAVOR AND ARE GREAT FOR THE BODY; THEY HAVE THREE TIMES MORE IRON THAN BROCCOLI AND HAVE BEEN SHOWN TO BOOST IMMUNE SYSTEM FUNCTION.

3 sunchokes
1 green apple
1 tbsp (15 g) ginger

Wash, peel and chop the produce as needed, removing any seeds from the fruit. Juice.

ENERGIZER BUNNY

ONE OF MY FIRST ANIMAL COMPANIONS, A RABBIT WHOM I NAMED COTTONTAIL, WAS ALWAYS BEGGING ME TO FEED HER CRUNCHY CARROTS AND JUICY CELERY. MUNCHING ON THEM ALL DAY WAS HER IDEA OF PARADISE. SHE HAD GREAT INSTINCTS! BOTH OF THESE FOODS ARE TERRIFIC FOR YOUR ENTIRE BODY, AS WELL AS SUPER HYDRATING. I'M SAVING MYSELF THE MUNCHING STEP AND THROWING THEM RIGHT THROUGH THE JUICER FOR FASTER NUTRIENT ABSORPTION. LET'S BOUNCE.

5 celery sticks
5 large carrots

Wash, peel and chop the carrots and celery as needed, then put them through your juicer, alternating between the two and going slowly (carrots can be tough to juice sometimes). Enjoy!

SAVORY BEETS

I'VE SAID IT BEFORE AND I WILL SAY IT AGAIN: I LOVE THE EARTHY FLAVOR OF BEETS. THOSE TONES GO GREAT WITH GARLIC AND GINGER, AND THAT IS PRETTY MUCH WHAT THIS JUICE IS. IT'S A NICE ONE FOR MID-MORNING, IN MY HUMBLE OPINION.

2 beets
1 tbsp (15 g) ginger
1 garlic clove
2 carrots

Wash, peel and chop the produce as needed. Put everything through your juicer, alternating the beets with the other ingredients, and enjoy!

ONE LOVE LETTUCE

THIS RECIPE IS PRETTY GREEN, SO I RECOMMEND GETTING USED TO LESS-SWEET JUICES BEFORE MAKING IT SO YOU DON'T THINK IT'S TOO BITTER TO DRINK. HAVING SAID THAT, ONCE YOU GET ACCUSTOMED—IT IS DELICIOUS!

2 heads lettuce
1 cucumber
5 celery sticks
1 lemon
1 green apple

Wash, peel and chop the produce as needed, removing any seeds from the fruit. Juice it all!

BET YOUR BORSCHT

PRETTY UNIQUE FLAVORS GOING ON IN THIS ONE….

3 beets
½ head red cabbage
1 bunch dill
1 garlic clove
1 red apple

Wash, peel and chop the produce as needed, removing any seeds from the fruit. Juice it up. Drink it down.

WHEATGRASS SHOTS

POTENT AND POWERFUL, YOU DON'T NEED MUCH! DRINK THESE ON AN EMPTY STOMACH TO GET THE MOST BENEFITS. YOU CAN BUY WHEATGRASS TRAYS AT SOME HEALTH FOOD STORES, OR GROW YOUR OWN FOR CHEAP! JUST SEARCH IT ON THE INTERNET TO LEARN HOW. YOU ALSO NEED A HIGH-QUALITY JUICER TO SUCCESSFULLY JUICE WHEATGRASS—CHECK OUT THE BRANDS I RECOMMEND ON PAGE 194.

1 tray wheatgrass 21" x 11" x 2" (53 x 28 x 5 cm)

Cut the grass near the root, rinse it off and then put through your juicer...time for shots!

CHAPTER 3

SWEET SMOOTHIES

Delicious any time of day (especially for breakfast), the smoothie recipes in this chapter are perfect for providing quickly absorbed energy and fantastic flavor. Sweet fruits are a key to long-term health and wellness; they contain incredible amounts of antioxidants that have been proven to prevent and fight cancer and a plethora of other chronic diseases and illnesses. They are also very high in water content (making them super hydrating) and essential vitamins, minerals and nutrients. The majority of my diet is sweet fruits; they are the ideal food for humans because of the balance of their water content, calorie count, nutritional density and amount of fiber. There are no bad fruits!

If you have trouble getting all of your 5–10 recommended servings of fruit in on a daily basis, then this is the chapter for you. In one colorful and tasty glass, you can sip up all that goodness in minutes and get on with the day. Having said that, 5–10 fruits a day is still on the low side in my opinion. Try to get in as many fruits and vegetables as possible every-day: the more, the better. These smoothies are full of juicy, sweet fruits, making them really easy for all to enjoy. Trying to get your kids to eat healthier? Hand them a Mint Cacao Kiss (page 112) and they'll be pleading for seconds.

All of these would be great for post-workout nutrition because they are full of good carbs that your body requires after cardio-vascular exercise. If you're working out for a longer period of time and using weights, simply throw in a scoop of your favorite plant-based protein powder (I love Vega), and your muscles will thank you.

THE BASIC GREEN

THIS COULD ALSO BE CALLED "THE ESSENTIAL SMOOTHIE" BECAUSE IT'S JUST THAT. IT IS INFINITELY ADAPTABLE SO YOU CAN CHANGE IT UP EVERY DAY WHILE STILL FOLLOWING THE SAME FUNDAMENTAL RECIPE. INSTEAD OF SPINACH, USE ANY DARK LEAFY GREENS; INSTEAD OF STRAWBERRIES, USE ANY FROZEN FRUIT; AND INSTEAD OF MYLK, USE ANY LIQUID (LIKE WATER OR FRESH JUICE)! I DRINK THIS EVERY MORNING AFTER I EXERCISE; IT IS WHAT MY BODY CRAVES. HAVE FUN! GET SEXY!

2 bananas
3 cups (675 g) spinach
1 cup (150 g) frozen strawberries
2 cups (470 mL) basic mylk (page 160)

Blend until smooth...ahh. Big smile.

APPLE CINNAMON DELIGHT

THIS TASTES LIKE APPLE PIE IN A MUG. ENOUGH SAID? YEP.

3 large apples, seeds removed
3 bananas
2 tsp (5 g) cinnamon
1 tsp (2 g) nutmeg
1-2 cups (240-470 mL) spiced mylk (page 163)

Blend all the ingredients together until smooth and creamy, adding spices as desired. Sprinkle some cinnamon on top and enjoy.

GRAPEFRUIT MANGO IMMUNE BOOSTER

DON'T WANT TO GET A COLD? DRINK THIS. ALL THE INGREDIENTS ARE VERY HIGH IN VITAMIN C, WHICH ACTS AS A NATURAL ANTIHISTAMINE AND HAS BEEN PROVEN TO HELP PREVENT COLDS AS WELL AS SHORTEN THEIR DURATION. IT IS ALSO HIGH IN ANTIOXIDANTS THAT FIGHT EVERYTHING FROM CANCER TO CATARACTS TO HIGH BLOOD PRESSURE. IF YOU LIKE THE FLAVOR OF GRAPEFRUIT, YOU'LL LOVE THIS ONE.

1 cup (151 g) frozen mango
1 cup (165 g) pineapple
1 grapefruit
1 cup (237 mL) water

Slice all the rind off the grapefruit. Blend all ingredients together until smooth and orange-pinkish. Gulp down the goodness.

GINGER PEPPERMINT LIVER CLEANSER

PEPPERMINT LEAVES HELP YOUR LIVER BY INCREASING BILE FLOW WHILE BREAKING DOWN FATS AND LOWERING BAD CHOLESTEROL. GINGER HAS BEEN PROVEN TO PREVENT DISEASES ASSOCIATED WITH THE LIVER AS WELL AS CLEANSE THE BLOOD. HEALTH BENEFITS ASIDE, THE FLAVORS COMBINE WITH TROPICAL FRUITS TO MAKE ONE DELICIOUSLY FRESH DRINK. HAVE THIS ONE IN THE MORNING TO START YOUR DAY OFF RIGHT.

1 cup (24 g) packed mint leaves
2 bananas
4 ice cubes
1 tbsp (15 g) ginger
1 cup (165 g) pineapple
1–3 cups (237-710 mL) water

Blend all ingredients until smooth and green, making sure there aren't any fibers from the ginger left unblended...they get in your teeth.

BERRY BERRY BEAR HUG

THEY MIGHT LOOK FEROCIOUS, BUT NORMALLY A BEAR'S IDEA OF A PERFECT DAY IS NIBBLING ON BERRIES IN THE QUIET FOREST; I CAN RELATE. THIS SMOOTHIE IS BURSTING WITH BLUEBERRIES AND STRAWBERRIES, AS WELL AS SOME WALNUTS, BANANAS AND FRESH VANILLA BEAN. SHARE THE LOVE!

2 cups (310 g) frozen blueberries
2 cups (298 g) frozen strawberries
2 bananas
1 cup (236 mL) water
¼ cup (29 g) walnuts
½ vanilla bean

Blend it up until smooth and frosty. Drink.

BANANA SPINACH ALMOND DREAM

IF YOU DON'T WANT TO EAT A GIANT BAG OF SPINACH EVERY DAY—BUT KNOW YOU SHOULD BE CONSUMING MORE GREENS—TRY THIS RECIPE OUT. THE FRESH ALMOND MYLK AND BANANAS BALANCE OUT THE SPINACH AND CREATE A CREAMY, SWEET DRINK THAT ALSO COUNTS AS A GIANT SALAD!

2 bananas
1 cup (165 g) frozen pineapple
2 cups (273 mL) basic mylk (page 160)
4 cups (120 g) spinach
1 orange

Remove the seeds from the orange. Blend up everything until smooth and evenly colored (it'll be a vibrant green). Slurp!

SPIRULINA POWER

I LOVE DRINKING THIS SMOOTHIE RIGHT AFTER A WORKOUT TO NOURISH MY MUSCLES. SPIRULINA (GREEN ALGAE) IS PACKED WITH PROTEIN, VITAMIN B2, COPPER AND IRON: ALL OF THESE WORK TO REBUILD MUSCLE TISSUE AND GIVE YOU ENERGY FOR THE REST OF THE DAY! IT HELPS RID HEAVY METALS AND OTHER BODILY WASTE FROM THE SYSTEM. DON'T BE INTIMIDATED BY THE COLOR OF SPIRULINA POWDER…THAT DARK GREEN MEANS IT'S FULL OF CHLOROPHYLL (AN AMAZING BLOOD CLEANSER AND CANCER-FIGHTING MOLECULE).

2 oranges
1 cup (165 g) pineapple
2 bananas
5 ice cubes
1 tbsp (1 g) spirulina powder

Blend until smooth. Enjoy.

BERRY CITRUS BLITZ

I RECOMMEND USING A BERRY MEDLEY IN THIS RECIPE FOR A LARGER VARIETY OF BENEFITS AND FLAVORS. ALTHOUGH I BELIEVE ALL PLANTS WERE CREATED EQUAL… BLUEBERRIES ARE SHAMELESSLY MY FAVORITE. I WAIT ALL YEAR FOR OUR BUSHES TO BLOSSOM, AND MY DIET IN THE SUMMER ENDS UP BEING LARGELY BLUEBERRIES. BERRIES HAVE BEEN PRAISED FOR AGES ON THEIR AMAZING ANTIOXIDANT CONTENT (THEY'RE BASICALLY CANCER-FIGHTING SUPERHEROES) AS WELL AS THEIR HIGH PERCENTAGE OF FIBER AND IMMUNE BOOSTER VITAMIN C, BONE-BUILDING VITAMIN K AND MANGANESE.

2 bananas
2 oranges
1 cup (155 g) frozen berries
1 cup (237 mL) basic mylk (page 160)

Blend until it's all smooth. Sip and enjoy. *Ahhh.*

ALMOST
A STRAWBERRY
MYLKSHAKE

LIKE THE NAME SAYS, THIS IS PRETTY DANG CLOSE TO A STRAWBERRY MYLKSHAKE (PAGE 166) AS FAR AS FLAVOR AND COLOR GO. MAKE IT, SHAKE IT, DRANK IT.

2 bananas
1 orange
1 cup (149 g) frozen strawberries
2 cups (473 mL) basic mylk (page 160)

Blend. Slurp. *Mmm.*

ALMOST A STRAWBERRY MYLKSHAKE... PLUS SPIRULINA!

IN OTHER WORDS: ALL THE SAME BENEFITS, AND IT'S GREEN.

2 bananas
1 orange
1 cup (149 g) frozen strawberries
2 cups (473 mL) basic mylk (page 160)
1 tbsp (5 g) spirulina powder
1 tbsp (10 g) hemp seeds

Blend everything together until it's evenly dark green.

GREEN GINGER PEAR JOY

I MADE THIS RECIPE ONE MORNING FOR MY BEAU BEFORE WE SET OUT ON A DAY OF ADVENTURING; I COULD NOT HAVE BLENDED UP A BETTER START! IT'S SWEET, FLAVORFUL AND FULL OF LIFE. IF YOU LOVE SPINACH, PEARS AND GINGER—YOU WILL ADORE THIS SMOOTHIE. NOTE: IF YOU DON'T HAVE FROZEN PEAR SLICES ON HAND, YOU CAN JUST USE FRESH PEAR AND ADD A FEW ICE CUBES.

2 tbsp (29 g) ginger
2 oranges
2 pitted dates
2 cups (346 g) frozen pear slices
4 cups (120 g) spinach
2 cups (473 mL) water

Peel the ginger and oranges and pit the dates. Throw everything into the blender and whizz it up until smooth and bright green. Woo!

TROPIKALE ENERGIZER

WITH PLENTY OF CITRUS, VITAMIN C, POTASSIUM, FIBER AND HEALTHY CARBS, THIS DRINK WILL GIVE YOU ENERGY FOR HOURS. THIS IS TYPICALLY WHAT I MAKE MOST MORNINGS AFTER YOGA AND MAN OH MAN IT MAKES ME FEEL SUNNY FROM THE INSIDE OUT (I MEAN THAT IN A GOOD WAY).

2 bananas
2 oranges
1 cup (165 g) frozen pineapple
1 cup (67 g) kale
2 pitted dates
2 cups (473 mL) water

Blend everything up until smooth and a vibrant green color. Sip in the sunshine!

MELLOW YELLOW

THIS IS ONE OF MY FAVE RECIPES BECAUSE IT'S SWEET, SIMPLE AND ABSOLUTELY BURSTING WITH VITAMIN C. DRINK THIS IF YOU FEEL A COLD COMING ON…OR EVERY DAY JUST BECAUSE IT TASTES GREAT AND YOUR BODY WANTS IT!

1 cup (155 g) frozen mango
2 bananas
1 cup (165 g) pineapple
1 orange
1 cup (237 mL) basic mylk (page 160)

Blend all the ingredients until smooth and glowing yellow. Well…not literally glowing.

GINGER CILANTRO MANGO ELIXIR

THIS IS BOTH REFRESHING AND CLEANSING. GINGER AND CILANTRO ARE AMAZING FOR YOUR BLOOD, AND THEY TASTE DELICIOUS PAIRED WITH SWEET TROPICAL FRUITS LIKE MANGO AND BANANA.

1 cup (25 g) cilantro leaves
1 green apple, seeded
1 tbsp (15 g) ginger
1 cup (237 mL) water
½ cucumber
1 frozen banana
1 cup (155 g) frozen mango

Blend everything up until smooth and green. Drink it!

MACA BLUEBERRY BLESSING

ONE OF MY ALL-TIME FAVORITES, THIS SMOOTHIE GIVES OFF ALL KINDS OF ORGANIC LOVE VIBES. IT'S VIBRANT IN COLOR, NUTRIENTS AND TASTE! MACA AND COCONUT WATER ADD EXTRA BENEFITS INCLUDING ELECTROLYTES, MAKING THIS RECIPE A GREAT CHOICE DURING EXERCISE. I THINK I'M A BLUEBERRY ADDICT. THAT'S A LEGITIMATE CONDITION, RIGHT?

1 cup (155 g) frozen blueberries
1 banana
2 oranges, seeded
1 tbsp (5 g) maca powder
2 cups (473 mL) coconut water

Blend everything up until smooth and beautifully purple. Enjoy.

CITRUS MANGO SAMBA

THIS SMOOTHIE IS GONNA MAKE YOU WANNA GET UP AND SHAKE YOUR TAIL FEATHER, ESPECIALLY IF YOU'RE ALREADY LISTENING TO SOME GOOD OLE MUNGO JERRY. THE CITRUS ADDS A BIT OF TARTNESS, BUT THE SWEETNESS FROM THE MANGO BALANCES IT ALL OUT.

1 cup (155 g) frozen mango
1 grapefruit, seeded
1 lemon, seeded
1 orange
1 cup (237 mL) water

Blend everything together until smooth. Drink! Dance!

PINEAPPLE BERRY MIXER

I LOVE PINEAPPLE IN SMOOTHIES—IT IS SUPER SWEET AND AT THE SAME TIME IT GIVES YOU A LITTLE BIT OF TARTNESS. YOU MAY NOT KNOW THIS BECAUSE IT SEEMS COUNTERINTUITIVE, BUT TART FRUITS LIKE LEMONS AND PINEAPPLE ACTUALLY BECOME ALKALIZING (NOT ACIDIC) ONCE THEY ENTER YOUR SYSTEM—HUH! ALKALIZING FOODS KEEP YOUR BLOOD HEALTHY. EAT MORE OF THEM.

1 cup (240 g) pineapple
⅓ cup (51 g) frozen blueberries
⅓ cup (51 g) frozen raspberries
⅓ cup (50 g) frozen mulberries
1 cup (237 mL) basic mylk (page 160)

Blend it all up until smooth and a vibrant deep purple. Enjoy.

MINT CACAO KISS

I CALLED THIS ONE A KISS BECAUSE IT'S LIGHT, SWEET AND YOU'RE PROBABLY GOING TO FALL IN LOVE WITH IT, OR AT LEAST SHARE IT WITH SOMEONE YOU ALSO SHARE KISSES WITH. PEPPERMINT IS GREAT FOR TAMING AN UPSET TUMMY, AND WHEN THE CREAMY GREEN SMOOTHIE IS PAIRED WITH CRUNCHY, BITTER CACAO NIBS, YOU'VE GOT ONE CUP OF "HOLY DELICIOUS!"

1 cup (24 g) mint leaves
1 orange
2 frozen bananas
1 cup (237 mL) spiced mylk (page 163)
1 tbsp (11 g) cacao nibs

Blend everything together (except the cacao nibs) until smooth and green and top off with the nibs. Crunch!

VANILLA MELON MAGIC

THE DELICIOUSNESS OF THIS RECIPE CAUGHT ME OFF GUARD; I WAS EXPECTING IT TO TASTE GOOD, BUT IT TOTALLY BLEW MY MIND BEYOND THAT! IT'S LIKE A FRUITY VANILLA MYLKSHAKE! KIDS AND ADULTS ALIKE WILL LOVE THIS ONE.

1 cantaloupe (about 3 cups [531 g])
1 cup (155 g) frozen mango
1 tsp vanilla powder

Spoon out the fruit of the cantaloupe and put in a blender with the mango and vanilla—blend it all until smooth, creamy and thick. *Mmm!*

DRINK
FOR BEAUTY

ALL THE INGREDIENTS IN THIS RECIPE DO AMAZING THINGS FOR YOUR SKIN (IT'S YOUR LARGEST ORGAN, BY THE WAY, SO WE GOTTA TAKE CARE OF IT).

1 cup (155 g) frozen blueberries
1 cup (237 mL) coconut kefir
1 cup (245 g) almond yogurt
1 tbsp (28 g) lucuma powder
1 orange
1/16 tsp stevia powder

Blend everything together until smooth and creamy.

PIÑA COLADA

I'LL HAVE ONE STRAIGHT UP, THANKS. NOTE: REFRIGERATE THE PINEAPPLE OVERNIGHT BEFORE MAKING THIS IF YOU WANT IT TO BE COLD.

1 pineapple
¼ cup (60 mL) coconut milk (optional)

Cut off the skin, chop up the fruit and blend until smooth, adding the coconut milk if you're using it. Yep. That's it.

APPLES AND BANANAS

I LIKE TO EAT 'EM. OR IN THIS CASE…DRINK 'EM.

2 apples, seeds removed
2 frozen bananas
½ cup (120 g) spinach
1 cup (237 mL) basic mylk (page 160)

Remove the seeds from the apples and blend everything up until smooth.

MANGO COCONUT LASSI

THIS IS AN AMAZING DRINK. IT IS CREAMY, SWEET AND TAKES MY MIND TO SOMEWHERE TROPICAL AND WARM...I COULD PROBABLY DRINK THIS EVERY DAY. MAKE IT FOR INDIAN NIGHT!

2 cups (310 g) frozen mango
2 cups (490 g) coconut yogurt
1 cup (237 mL) coconut milk
1 tbsp (21 g) coconut nectar

Blend everything until smooth, thick and creamy. Enjooooy.

HIP HIP HYDRATION

ALTHOUGH ALL THE RECIPES IN THIS BOOK ARE GREAT FOR KEEPING YOUR BODY HYDRATED, THE CUCUMBER IN THIS ONE GOES THE EXTRA MILE (OR KILOMETER, SINCE I'M CANADIAN).

1 cup (67 g) kale
1 cup (155 g) frozen mango
½ cucumber
1⁄16 tsp stevia powder
1–2 cups (237–473 mL) water

Blend everything until smooth, green and creamy!

LUCUMA LUXE

THE COLOR AND FLAVOR OF THIS RECIPE SEEMS VERY ELEGANT, ALMOST ROYAL, TO ME.
MAKE THIS SMOOTHIE AND SEE IF YOU AGREE.

1 cup (155 g) frozen berries
1 banana
1 mango
1 tbsp (28 g) lucuma powder
1 cup (237 mL) water

Blend all the ingredients until smooth.

YUMBERRY LOVE

YUMBERRIES HAVE HISTORICALLY BEEN GROWN AND ENJOYED IN CHINA FOR A LOOONG TIME, AND WITH GOOD REASON. THESE BERRIES HAVE A UNIQUELY SWEET AND TART TASTE, AND PROVIDE HUGE AMOUNTS OF POLYPHENOLS AND ANTHOCYANINS; THEY ARE ALSO KNOWN TO HELP WITH LIVER FUNCTION, SKIN COMPLEXION AND EYESIGHT.

1 cup (155 g) frozen mango
1 cup (240 g) pineapple
½ cucumber
1 tbsp (28 g) yumberry powder
1 cup (237 mL) water

Blend everything until smooth. Feel the love.

SEA BUCKTHORN SWEETNESS

SEA BUCKTHORN GROWS IN THE DESERTS OF EUROPE AND ASIA WHERE IT MUST DEFEND ITSELF AGAINST THE HARSH CLIMATES, CAUSING IT TO HAVE COUNTLESS ANTIOXIDANTS AND BIOACTIVE COMPONENTS THAT ARE GREAT FOR US!

2 bananas
2 oranges
6 ice cubes
1 tbsp (28 g) sea buckthorn powder

Blend it all up.

CHIA BUBBLE TEA

MY FRIEND, ANOTHER EMILY, GAVE ME THE IDEA FOR THIS RECIPE. I KNOW PEOPLE LOVE BUBBLE TEA, SO I MADE A HEALTHY VERSION.

½ cup (83 g) pineapple
1 cup (237 mL) basic mylk (page 160)
2 frozen bananas
1 orange
2 tbsp (16 g) chia seeds

Blend everything except the chia seeds until smooth and yellow. Pour the chia seeds into the bottom of a glass, then fill 'er on up with the smoothie.

PEPPERMINT CUCUMBER REFRESHER

MY PARTNER AND I ENJOYED THIS IN A SUNNY BACKYARD AFTER A STRESSFUL DAY AND IT CALMED US BOTH RIGHT DOWN; I WENT FROM BEING EXTREMELY GLUM, SORE AND TIRED TO FEELING MY BEST. CLEARLY, THIS DRINK HAS SECRET MAGICAL PROPERTIES.

½ cucumber (you can leave the skin on if it's organic)
2 frozen bananas
½ cup (12 g) mint leaves
1 cup (165 g) pineapple
⅟₁₆ tsp stevia powder
2 cups (473 mL) water

Blend everything until smooth and green. *Ahhh.*

ANTI-INFLAMMATORY SMOOTHIE

AFTER A TOUGH WORKOUT, MY MUSCLES GET SORE. CUE…THIS RECIPE! ALL THE INGREDIENTS ARE HELPFUL WITH—YOU GUESSED IT—RELIEVING THE DISCOMFORT OF SORE MUSCLES AND INFLAMED TISSUE.

1 cup (155 g) pitted cherries
1 cup (155 g) frozen blueberries
1 tbsp (15 g) ginger
2 oranges
1 cup (237 mL) water

Blend everything together until smooth and dark reddish/blue. Drink.

BOLD AND GOLD

MORE OF A LIGHT YELLOW THAN GOLD, BUT I GOT YOUR ATTENTION.

2 frozen bananas
3 apples, seeds removed
4 pineapple slices
2 cups (473 mL) water

Blend until smooth and gold (er...yellow-ish).

BLUEBERRYLICIOUS SMOOTHIE

I CAN'T HANDLE THE DELICIOUSNESS (LET ALONE THE BERRYLICIOUSNESS).

1 cup (155 g) frozen blueberries
4 bananas
6 pitted dates
2 cups (473 mL) basic mylk (page 160)

Blend until smooth and creamy. *Mmm*, oh yes.

SWEET CHERRY ALMOND SMOOTHIE

THIS TASTES EVEN BETTER THAN IT SOUNDS.

1 cup (155 g) frozen cherries
1 orange
1 cup (237 mL) basic mylk (page 160) made with almonds
3 pitted dates
1 banana

Blend it all up and slurp it down!

SMOOTHIE FOR YOUR SWEETHEART

I ACTUALLY DID MAKE THIS ONE FOR MY HONEYBUN (HE WOULD NOT APPROVE OF MY CALLING HIM THAT, SO LET'S KEEP IT ON THE DOWN LOW) WHEN WE WERE ON A JUICE AND SMOOTHIE CLEANSE, AND WE BOTH LOVED IT.

2 bananas
2 apples, seeds removed
4 pineapple slices
½ cup (78 g) frozen berries
2 cups (473 mL) water

Blend until smooth and pink!

THE OGOPOGO

SUPPOSEDLY IN THE OKANOGAN VALLEY, THERE IS A LAKE WHERE A MYTHICAL SEA CREATURE LIVES, AND ITS FOLK NAME IS OGOPOGO (BC'S VERY OWN LOCH NESS MONSTER). THE INGREDIENTS IN THIS SMOOTHIE ARE SYMBOLS OF THE OKANOGAN'S FERTILE SOIL AND FARMS, AND I LOOK FORWARD TO SEEING THESE ICONIC FRUITS EVERY SUMMER AT FARMERS MARKETS.

2 peaches
1 cup (155 g) cherries, pitted
2 apples, seeds removed
1 cup (237 mL) basic mylk (page 160)

Blend everything up until smooth (make sure you pit the peaches!) and sip while contemplating what good ole Ogopogo is up to....

CHAPTER 4

SAVORY SMOOTHIES

The main ingredients in these recipes are non-sweet fruits (like cucumbers, tomatoes and bell peppers) and vegetables (like broccoli, carrots and onions). These foods are super low in calories while at the same time being amazingly micro- and macro-nutrient dense. For example, calorie for calorie, spinach has more protein than steak. Go plants! Popeye knew what was up.

Non-sweet fruits and vegetables are excellent foods for filling up on and getting a more than sufficient amount of vitamins, minerals and nutrients. This is because they contain enormous amounts of fiber, which give you the feeling of satiation. Many of these smoothie recipes also contain nuts and seeds for added nutritional benefits and to make the smoothie a legitimate meal.

If the idea of a savory smoothie is weird or unappealing to you, think of these recipes as soups; pour them in a bowl and top them off with chopped veggies and herbs. Ta-da! Healthy, flavorful bowls of fresh delight in just a few minutes. Or use these recipe as sauces: Pour them over brown rice and steamed veggies for an amazingly healthy and filling meal. The recipes in this chapter are great for lunch or dinner when you want to add in some extra, cleansing nutrition or when you simply don't feel like cooking. Just as sweet fruit smoothies are the perfect start to your day, savory veggie smoothies are the ideal meal when you're winding down.

Note: If ya wanna keep these recipes totally raw, skip the cooking part (except for the Creamy Onion and Potato Smoothie, page 155)! Simple. But keep in mind, it is creamier if you let the veggies simmer.

CREAMY BROCCOLI WITH GARLIC AND CILANTRO

THIS IS A FANTASTIC, FLAVORFUL GREEN BLEND FOR LUNCH OR DINNER. I PREFER TO THINK OF THIS RECIPE AS CREAMY BROCCOLI SOUP WITH GARLIC, HERBS AND SPICES. ENJOY IT FROM A GLASS WITH A STRAW OR IN A BOWL WITH A SPOON! HOWEVER IT GETS IN YOU, IT'S GONNA DO GOOD THINGS.

2 cups (142 g) broccoli

1 garlic clove

2 tbsp (17 g) miso paste

1 orange

¼ cup (43 g) almonds

¼ cup (38 g) pitted dates

½ tsp coriander

½ tsp paprika

½ tsp turmeric

1 cup (16 g) cilantro

1½ cups (355 mL) water, as needed

1 avocado (optional, but if you do use it remember to remove the pit)

Peel, wash and chop everything as needed. Blend all the ingredients together, adding water as needed.

CURRIED CARROT CREAM

THIS IS VIRTUALLY FAT-FREE AND YET SO CREAMY AND FLAVORFUL! I LIKE TO THINK OF IT AS CARROT SOUP…I LOVE EATING IT WITH A SPOON AND HOW IT WARMS ME RIGHT UP WITH WHOLESOME GOODNESS. TRY IT FOR LUNCH OR DINNER.

5 large carrots
1 onion
3 garlic cloves ·
4 cups (946 mL) vegetable broth
Salt, pepper and curry powder to taste

Wash, peel and chop the veggies and put them in a pot with the broth. Bring to a boil, then reduce to a simmer and keep it that way until the carrots are soft. Let the mixture cool down for about 30-60 minutes then blend until smooth and creamy, adding the salt, pepper and curry powder as desired. The taste is gonna blow your mind!

KINDA LIKE TOMATO SOUP SMOOTHIE

OBVIOUSLY, I HAD TROUBLE THINKING OF A NAME FOR THIS ONE. IN ANY CASE, IT'S FREAKING DELICIOUS. MY FAVE WAY TO EAT IT? AS A SAUCE WITH RICE AND VEGGIES.

1 cup (160 g) tomatoes
1 avocado
1 tbsp (17 g) miso paste
Cumin, coriander, Himalayan salt and pepper (to taste)
1 cup (237 mL) water
1 garlic clove

Blend everything until smooth and light red or orange-y, adding spices as desired. Serve with extra chopped avocado and cherry tomatoes!

TOMATO GARLIC SMOOTHIE WITH ONIONS AND SPICES

THIS IS A DELIGHTFULLY TANGY, SAVORY AND FLAVORFUL RECIPE THAT IS PERFECT FOR DINNER WHEN YOU DON'T FEEL LIKE EATING SOMETHING HEAVY OR MAKING SOMETHING COMPLICATED.

2 cups (322 g) tomatoes
1 garlic clove
⅛ cup (25 g) onion
1 red bell pepper, seeds removed
1 avocado
Pinch Himalayan salt
1 tsp cumin
1 tsp coriander
1–2 cups (237-473 mL) water or vegetable broth

Blend everything until smooth. Serve with cilantro if ya want.

THE BEST CORN AND CAULIFLOWER SMOOTHIE

I FIRST CREATED THIS RECIPE WHILE DOING A LIQUID CLEANSE WITH MY PARTNER AND I REMEMBER IT TASTING BEYOND AMAZING—IT TOTALLY HIT THE SPOT THAT NIGHT. NOW MY MOUTH IS WATERING JUST THINKING ABOUT IT.

1 head cauliflower
2 cups (272 g) corn
6 field tomatoes
1 avocado
Juice from ½ lime
1 garlic clove
2 tbsp (33 g) miso paste
Cumin and coriander, to taste
Hot water, as needed

Steam the cauliflower and corn until tender (or leave it raw if that is important to you), then put everything in your blender. Blend until smooth, adding water in ½ cup (118 mL) amounts until you have your desired consistency. This makes a lot. It should taste amazing. If it doesn't, adjust according to taste until you like what you've got.

MEXICO-INSPIRED SMOOTHIE

I HAVE A DEAR FRIEND WHO OWNS AN AMAZING RESTAURANT IN MÉRIDA, YUCATAN; HE IS THE INSPIRATION FOR THIS RECIPE, SINCE HE ALWAYS MAKING ME DROOL WHEN HE DESCRIBES THE ABUNDANCE OF FRESH FRUITS AND VEGGIES THEY HAVE THERE.

5 tomatoes
2 cups (272 g) corn
1 avocado
Juice from ½ lime
1 tsp coriander
Pepper, to taste
Vegetable broth, as needed

Blend everything until smooth, adding the veggie broth in ½ cup (118 mL) amounts until you have your desired consistency.

SPICY CARROT SMOOTHIE WITH BELL PEPPERS

CREAMY, VIBRANT, CAROTENE-PACKED BLISS IN A BOWL.

4 cups (512 g) carrots
1 onion
2 orange bell peppers
3 small tomatoes
Cumin and coriander, to taste
1 tsp lemon juice
3 pitted dates
Vegetable broth or water, enough to cover veggies in a pot

Roughly chop all the veggies. Cover the carrots and onions with vegetable broth or water in a pot and bring to a boil. Reduce heat to low and let them cook for about 30 minutes or until tender. Throw all the ingredients (including the veggie broth mix) into a high-speed blender and blend until smooth and creamy, adding the spices as you like. Serve with tomato slices and cilantro if you want!

CREAMY ONION AND POTATO SMOOTHIE

I COULDN'T BELIEVE HOW FABULOUS THIS TASTED THE FIRST TIME I WHIPPED IT UP. THIS RECIPE IS OIL-FREE AND SALT-FREE BUT IT IS JUST AS SATISFYING—IF NOT MORE SO, SINCE IT'S SO HEALTHY—AS YOUR REGULAR POTATO SOUP (WHICH IS USUALLY LADEN WITH BUTTER AND SALT)!

6 potatoes
1 onion
2 garlic cloves
Enough vegetable broth to cover the potatoes and onions
1 tsp coriander
1 tsp dill
1 tsp fresh parsley

Slice the veggies then cover with the broth and bring to a boil. Reduce to a simmer and let cook until tender, around 25 minutes. Put everything into your blender and blend until smooth. It is shockingly delicious! Add whatever else you like.

SPICY AVOCADO AVIATOR

SO. CREAMY.

1 avocado
½ cucumber (you can leave the skin on if it's organic)
1 tsp lime juice
1 cup (245 g) coconut yogurt
1 garlic clove
½ tsp Himalayan salt
½ tsp chili powder, to taste

Blend everything until smooth, adding the spice as desired! This is really tasty when you add chunks of mango.

CHAPTER 5

MYLKS & MYLKSHAKES

Why the "y"? No, it's not because I'm illiterate. Actually, I intentionally spell "mylk" in this book without the conventional "i" because all the recipes are dairy-free! If you currently consume dairy, before you freak out and stick your nose at me and my lack-of-lactose ways, lemme say a few things. Have you ever thought about why you are drinking the milk of another species when you are far past needing even your own mother's milk? It don't make no sense. Cow milk is for baby cows! On a more positive note, these non-dairy mylks have all the stuff you want from their cow-sourced counterparts, but I'd argue they're even better because no one gets hurt (if you think dairy is a harmless industry, I suggest you watch a documentary called *Earthlings* and check out page 198). The following recipes have all the calcium, vitamins, minerals, protein and deliciousness of regular milk, without the anitbiotics, unnatural sourcing, processing or freaky stabilizers or artificially added nutrients.

For all these mylk recipes, you can use nuts (like almonds, pecans and walnuts), seeds (such as pumpkin, hemp and sunflower) or coconut meat (dried or fresh). I recommend using raw nuts or seeds and soaking them in water for at least 6 hours so their vitamins and nutrients are more easily absorbed by your body. Then rinse them off with fresh water and you're ready to roll!

BASIC MYLK

SIMPLE AND DELICIOUS. PERFECT FOR ADDING TO SMOOTHIES, GRANOLA OR OATMEAL. USE ANY KIND OF NUT OR SEED YOU LIKE; EXAMPLES ARE ALMONDS, CASHEWS, PUMPKIN SEEDS, SUNFLOWER SEEDS, HEMP SEEDS, PECANS AND MACADAMIAS. YOU COULD EVEN USE COCONUT MEAT! THE NUT OR SEED YOU USE IN THIS RECIPE WILL DETERMINE THE FLAVOR OF THE MYLK. IF YOU LIKE CASHEWS, USE CASHEWS! IF PECANS ARE YOUR FAVE, TRY MAKING PECAN MYLK. THERE ARE ENDLESS POSSIBILITIES. PERSONALLY I LOVE WALNUTS, AND SO WALNUTS MYLK IS MY TOP PICK. ALSO KEEP IN MIND THAT SOME NUTS ALLOW FOR CREAMIER MYLK THAN OTHERS; CASHEWS, PINE NUTS AND MACADAMIAS ARE THE BEST FOR THIS BECAUSE OF THEIR HIGH HEALTHY FAT CONTENT.

MAKES: 4 CUPS (946 ML)

1 cup (100 g) raw nuts or seeds
3 cups (710 mL) water

Cover the nuts in water and let them soak for 6 hours. Discard the soak water and rinse the nuts with fresh water. Blend the soaked nuts with fresh water until smooth, frothy and white. Strain through a nut mylk bag or cheesecloth (or leave as is). Drink right away or store in the fridge in a sealable glass container for up to one week.

SPICED MYLK

THIS RECIPE IS SWEETENED WITH DATES AND MORE FLAVORFUL THAN THE BASIC ONE BECAUSE IT INCLUDES SPICES. ABSOLUTELY AMAZING ON ITS OWN OR ADDED TO OTHER RECIPES! I COULD DRINK THIS ALL DAY.

MAKES: 4½ CUPS (1 L)

1 cup (125 g) raw nuts, seeds or coconut meat
3 cups (237 mL) water
1 tsp cinnamon powder
½ tsp nutmeg powder
1 tsp vanilla extract
Pinch of pink Himalayan crystal salt
3–5 pitted dates

Cover the nuts or seeds (if using) in water and let them soak for 6 hours, then rinse and discard the soak water. Blend the soaked nuts, seeds or fresh coconut meat with the all the other ingredients until smooth, frothy and white. Strain through a nut mylk bag or cheesecloth (or leave as is). Store in the fridge in a sealable glass container for up to one week.

CHOCOLATE MYLK

CHOCOLATE. MYLK. NEED I SAY MORE?

MAKES: 4½ CUPS (1 L)

Follow the recipe for spiced mylk, adding 1–2 tablespoons (28–56 g) of cacao powder and, if you like, 1 tablespoon (28 g) of maca powder.

VANILLA MYLKSHAKE

SIMPLE, SUBLIME, SEXY: SIP IT UP.

MAKES: 4½ CUPS (1 L)

3 frozen bananas
1 cup (237 mL) basic mylk (page 160)
1 tsp vanilla powder
1 tsp vanilla extract
Pinch of Himalayan crystal salt
2-5 pitted dates

Blend it all up until thick and smooth. Pour into fancy glasses and savor with a straw...*mmm*.

CHOCOLATE MYLKSHAKE

THIS IS ABOUT AS DELICIOUS AND HEALTHFUL AS ANY MYLKSHAKE CAN POSSIBLY BE; DRINK IT UP AND FEEL GOOOOD. NO, SERIOUSLY. I DON'T THINK YOU UNDERSTAND HOW AMAZING THIS IS YET. MAKE IT ASAP.

MAKES: 3 CUPS (710 ML)

3 frozen bananas
1 cup (237 mL) basic mylk (page 160)
1 tsp vanilla powder
1 tbsp (28 g) cacao powder
¼ tsp cinnamon powder
¼ tsp cayenne powder
Pinch of Himalayan crystal salt
2-5 pitted dates

Blend it all up until thick and smooth. Add some cacao nibs for a crunch.

STRAWBERRY MYLKSHAKE

ALTHOUGH MY FAVORITE KIND OF MYLKSHAKE IS CHOCOLATE (I AM A SHAMELESSLY SELF-CONFESSED CHOCOHOLIC), I'M ALWAYS DELIGHTFULLY SURPRISED BY THE FRESH, FRUITY FLAVOR OF STRAWBERRY SHAKES. THEY MAKE ME THINK OF SUNNY SUMMERS IN THE BACKYARD.

MAKES: 5 CUPS (1.2 L)

3 frozen bananas
1 cup (237 mL) basic mylk (page 160)
1 tsp vanilla powder
Pinch of Himalayan crystal salt
2–5 pitted dates
1 cup (221 g) fresh or frozen strawberries

Blend it all up until thick and smooth. Garnish with sliced strawberries for extra color.

CREAMY ICED CHAI LATTE

WHO NEEDS A $7.00 FANCY DRINK FROM THE COFFEE SHOP WHEN YOU CAN MAKE YOUR OWN HEALTHY VERSION IN THE COMFORT OF YOUR KITCHEN? NOBODY I KNOW.

1 cup (237 mL) strong brewed chai tea
2 cups (473 mL) basic mylk (page 160)
1 tbsp (21 g) coconut nectar
1 cup (5 g) ice cubes

Let the tea cool down, then blend the tea, mylk and coconut nectar together and serve over ice. You could alternatively blend the ice into the drink, too.

CHAPTER 6

ENERGY BARS & HEALTHY SNACKS

These recipes for energy bars are perfect for staying satisfied in between meals, at the gym, in school or at work, and even as nutritious desserts. They contain ingredients like nuts, seeds, oats, dried fruit and other superfoods—but they are put together in creative ways that might make you feel surprised at how delicious healthy food can be! Don't be afraid of the fat content in nuts and seeds; the fats in these foods are excellent for your body and also necessary for you to survive! Fats function in the body to transport molecules, protect nerves and help brain function. Just keep in mind that you don't need much; your recommended daily intake is about ¼ cup (31 g) of nuts or seeds. My recipes don't go over that if you follow the serving suggestions. Also, don't be afraid of the sugars in dried fruit! Again, your body wants them. I suggest pairing these recipes with a glass of lemon water to keep your system hydrated, alkaline and nourished.

The recipes for snacks in this chapter are healthy solutions to those midday munchies that tempt many of us to hit up the vending machine for a bag of chips. Well I say: no more! Next time you're gonna be prepared with a big bag of crunchy Cheezy Garlic Kale Chips instead (page 192). Those vending machine folks will be staring longingly at your snack box while you happily munch away. Heh heh heeeh....

THE POWER BAR

THIS RECIPE HAS GOT EVERYTHING YOU NEED TO STAY ENERGIZED; WHILE YOU EXERCISE, WORK, PLAY OR PRACTICE WHATEVER OTHER ACTIVITIES FILL YOUR LIFE. NO NEED TO BUY EXPENSIVE, FANCY ENERGY BARS AT THE STORE—MAKE YOUR OWN! THEY ARE MORE AFFORDABLE, PROBABLY HEALTHIER AND TASTE BETTER!

MAKES: 8 BARS

⅓ cup (55 g) flax seeds, ground into flour
⅓ cup (27 g) rolled oats, ground into flour
¼ cup (16 g) pumpkin seeds
¼ cup (16 g) hemp seeds
1 cup (93 g) dried shredded coconut
1¼ cup (190 g) pitted dates
2 tbsp (27 g) melted coconut oil
1 tsp vanilla extract

Put everything into your food processor and process until it all sticks together. If it remains too crumbly, add more dates or coconut oil, or even some fresh lemon juice. Press into a lined 9 inch x 5 inch (23 x 13 cm) loaf pan and set in the fridge for about 3 hours. Garnish with more coconut shreds and pumpkin seeds, if you like. Slice into bars and enjoy! These will keep for about a week, but I am sure they'll be gone before that.

SEXY SEED MEDLEY

THIS RECIPE HAS THREE DIFFERENT SUPERFOOD SEEDS—HEMP, PUMPKIN AND CHIA—THAT ARE CHOCK FULL OF PROTEIN, FIBER, HEALTHY FATS, B VITAMINS, IRON, PHOSPHORUS AND POTASSIUM. KNOW WHAT ALL THOSE DO FOR YA? THEY GIVE YOU ENERGY AND STRENGTH, WHICH ALLOW YOU TO WORK HARD, LIVE LONG AND FEEL GOOD…THAT'S SEXY. ("AH, NOW I GET IT!")

MAKES: 8 BARS

1 cup (99 g) pecans
⅓ cup (48 g) chia seeds
⅓ cup (48 g) hemp seeds
⅓ cup (39 g) pumpkin seeds
2 cups (304 g) pitted dates
1 tsp vanilla extract
Pinch of Himalayan salt

Process the pecans into rough flour in a food processor. Add the rest of the ingredients and process until it all begins to stick together. Press into a lined 9 inch x 9 inch (23 x 23 cm) baking pan and let set in the fridge overnight, then cut into bars. Spread on peanut butter, drizzle on dark chocolate or sprinkle with dried fruit, coconut or cacao nibs.

COCO OAT BARS WITH PEANUT BUTTER AND CAROB

THESE ARE A GREAT SNACK TO BRING TO WORK, SCHOOL, TRAVELING OR ELSEWHERE BECAUSE THEY ARE EASY TO TRANSPORT AND PROVIDE DELICIOUSLY WHOLESOME ENERGY QUICK. THINK OF THEM AS A HEALTHY PEANUT BUTTER CHOCOLATE BAR.

MAKES: 6 BARS

BARS
1 cup (81 g) oats
½ cup (46 g) coconut shreds
⅓ cup (60 g) peanut butter
3 tbsp (40 g) melted coconut oil
1 tsp vanilla extract
Pinch of Himalayan salt

DATE PASTE
1 cup (152 g) pitted dates
¼-½ cup (60-120 mL) water, as needed
pinch of Himalayan salt

CAROB COATING
1 tbsp (13 g) melted coconut oil
1 tbsp (28 g) carob powder

Mix the bar ingredients together with a spoon until the oats are coated and you can press the mixture together. Press into the bottom of a lined baking pan and put in the fridge for an hour.

To make the date paste, blend everything together until smooth, adding water as needed to create a thick, creamy mixture. Alternatively you can make date syrup and add water until you have a more liquid consistency.

Mix the carob coating ingredients and date paste together in a bowl. Then, spread the carob coating onto the bars, slice and enjoy!

PEPPERMINT SPIRULINA BARS WITH CHOCOLATE FUDGE

THESE ARE FULL OF PROTEIN AND FIBER FROM THE OATS AND SPIRULINA, AND THE MACA BALANCES YOUR HORMONES—GREAT FOR AFTER A RUN OR TO KEEP YOU ENERGIZED BETWEEN MEALS.

MAKES: 16 BARS

CRUST
1 cup (81 g) oats
1 cup (152 g) pitted dates
1 tsp vanilla extract

PEPPERMINT SPIRULINA LAYER
1 cup (111 g) cashews
1 cup (152 g) pitted dates
3–4 tbsp (84–112 g) spirulina powder
2 tbsp (27 g) melted coconut oil

⅛ cup (3 g) packed mint leaves
Pinch of Himalayan salt
1 cup (237 mL) water, as needed

CHOCOLATE FUDGE
1 cup (152 g) pitted dates
1 cup (237 mL) water
2 tbsp (14 g) cacao powder
1 tbsp (7 g) maca powder
Cacao nibs and pumpkin seeds

To make the crust, pulse the oats into a powder in a food processor and add the dates and vanilla, processing until it all begins to stick together. Press into the bottom of a lined bread pan. Put in the fridge for 30 minutes so it hardens.

To make the peppermint spirulina layer, blend all the ingredients until smooth, adding as little water as possible. Spread onto your crust and put in the freezer until solid (about 2 hours).

To make the chocolate fudge, blend all the ingredients until smooth and thick. Spread onto your peppermint spirulina layer and leave in the fridge for 24–48 hours. Top with cacao nibs and pumpkin seeds, and slice.

DARK CHOCOLATE CHIP, OAT AND HEMP COOKIES

THESE COULD ALTERNATIVELY BE CALLED "OMG COOKIES" BECAUSE THAT WAS MY IMMEDIATE RESPONSE TO TASTING THEM. BETTER THAN ANY BAKED COOKIE I'VE EVER HAD, THE ONLY INGREDIENTS ARE HEALTHFUL, WHOLE FOODS THAT MAKE YOU FEEL AND LOOK FABULOUS.

MAKES: 10 HUGE COOKIES OR 20 NORMAL ONES

CHOCOLATE

2 tbsp (42 g) cacao powder
2 tbsp (27 g) melted coconut oil
1 tbsp (21 g) coconut nectar

COOKIES

2 cups (222 g) cashews
¾ cup (108 g) hemp seeds
1 cup (81 g) oats
¼ cup (85 g) coconut nectar
¼ cup (55 g) melted coconut oil
Pinch of Himalayan salt
1 tsp vanilla extract

To make the chocolate, whisk all the ingredients together until smooth. Pour into the bottom of a pan or on a plate and put in the freezer for 20 minutes or until solid, then cut or break apart into chocolate chip sized pieces.

To make the cookies, pulse the cashews and hemp seeds into powder in a food processor then add the rest of the ingredients and process until it all sticks together. Break up in a large bowl, then add the chocolate chips and mix everything together with your hands. Roll into cookies, or use an ice cream scoop. Drizzle with more chocolate if desired.

GREEN EARTH ORBS

THESE ORBS HAVE A DELICIOUS, DEEP NUTTY FLAVOR AND ARE POSITIVELY
PACKED WITH HEALTHY NUTS AND SEEDS THAT WILL MAKE YOUR SKIN GLOW AND
YOUR BODY SING!

MAKES: 15 ORBS

1 cup (31 g) walnuts
1 cup (64 g) pumpkin seeds
½ cup (72 g) chia seeds
1 cup (152 g) pitted dates
2 tbsp (27 g) coconut oil
¼ tsp Himalayan salt
1 tsp cinnamon

Pulse the nuts and seeds into powder in a food processor, then add the rest of the ingredients and process until it all begins to stick together. Try rolling a small handful into a ball. If it works, roll the rest of the mixture into balls. If it is still too crumbly, add more coconut oil or dates. Roll the balls in coconut and cinnamon for extra flavor and nutrition.

DARE TO DATE SQUARES

THESE SQUARES ARE AN EXCELLENT ENERGY BAR BECAUSE THEY'RE MOSTLY MADE UP OF DATES AND OATS, BOTH OF WHICH OF ARE FULL OF HEALTHY CARBS (BOTH SIMPLE AND COMPLEX) THAT WILL KEEP YOU FOCUSED AND FULL FOR HOURS! COMBINE THESE WITH FRUIT FOR AN AMAZING BREAKFAST, HAVE THEM ON THEIR OWN FOR A DELICIOUS AND QUICK SNACK OR EAT THEM AS A SUPER HEALTHY DESSERT! LIFE IS GOOD WHEN YOU'VE GOT A DATE (OR SEVERAL).

MAKES: 16 SQUARES

BASE
1 cup (81 g) rolled oats
1 cup (110 g) pecans
1 cup (152 g) pitted dates
1 tsp vanilla extract

MIDDLE
1½ cups (228 g) pitted dates
¼ cup (55 g) coconut oil

¼ tsp Himalayan salt
½ cup (118 mL) water, as needed

TOPPING
¼ cup (20 g) rolled oats
¼ cup (28 g) pecans
1 tbsp (14 g) coconut oil
Pinch Himalayan salt

To make the base, process the oats and pecans into flour in a food processor, then add the rest of the ingredients and process until it begins to stick together. Press into the bottom of a lined baking pan and put in the fridge.

To make the middle, put all the ingredients in your food processor and blend until smooth, adding water as needed in 1 tablespoon (15 mL) amounts to make it creamy, but keeping it thick enough so that it holds its shape. Spread evenly onto your base and put back in the fridge for about 30 minutes.

To make the topping, pulse all the ingredients in your food processor until they become a crumble-like consistency. Sprinkle evenly on top of the middle layer and press down lightly. Let the recipe sit in the fridge overnight so it can set and develop more flavor. Slice and enjoy!

ONION ROSEMARY FLAX BREAD

A CROSS BETWEEN BREAD AND CRACKERS, THIS RECIPE IS SUPER NUTRITIOUS AND FULL OF FIBER TO KEEP YOU NOURISHED AND SATISFIED. ENJOY IT WITH HUMMUS, NUT PATE OR PESTO AND LAYER WITH VEGGIES FOR A DELICIOUS MEAL, OR NIBBLE IT NAKED FOR A HEALTHY SNACK. MY FAVE WAY TO EAT THIS? WITH SOME KALE OLIVE TAPENADE, CUCUMBER AND TOMATO SLICES. OH—AND YOU GOTTA ADD AVOCADO. ALWAYS AVOCADO. FOREVER AVOCADO.

MAKES: 12 SLICES

1¼ cup (180 g) flax seeds
½ cup (76 g) onion
1 yellow bell pepper
1 tbsp (2 g) dried rosemary
1 tsp coriander
Salt and pepper, to taste

Grind 1 cup (144 g) of the flax seeds into flour in your blender. Combine with all the other ingredients, as well as the remaining flax, in a food processor and process until it becomes like a thick paste. Spread evenly into a 0.1 inch-0.2 inch (0.25-0.5 cm)-thick square on a dehydrator tray. Dehydrate for 1-2 hours then cut into squares and flip them over. Dehydrate for another 1-2 hours until pliable. Alternatively, you can use your oven at its lowest temperature, for about the same amount of time.

HIPPIE HEMP HUMMUS

MADE WITH HEMP SEED BUTTER INSTEAD OF THE TRADITIONAL SESAME SEED BUTTER, I DARE SAY I PREFER THIS VERSION TO THE ORIGINAL! I HAD TROUBLE STOPPING MYSELF FROM DEVOURING THE ENTIRE BOWL BEFORE I PHOTOGRAPHED IT. THIS TASTES PHENOMENAL WITH CARROTS, CUCUMBER, CELERY AND SUN-DRIED TOMATOES…AND PRETTY MUCH EVERYTHING ELSE.

MAKES: 3½ CUPS (793 G)

2 cups (304 g) cooked chickpeas
1 cup (250 g) hemp seed butter
¼ cup (54 g) extra virgin olive oil
1 tsp Himalayan salt
2 garlic cloves
½ tsp coriander
Juice from 1 lemon
Water, as needed

Put everything in the food processor and pulse until it becomes smooth (like hummus), adding water as needed in 1 tablespoon (15 mL) amounts to get the desired consistency. Adjust according to taste and then enjoy with fresh veggies!

CH-CH-CH-CHIA PUDDING

THE BASE OF THIS RECIPE IS CHIA SEEDS. THAT'S RIGHT, THE SAME PLANT THAT GROWS THE GRASS FOR CH-CH-CH-CHIA PETS IS ALSO ONE OF THE MOST NUTRITIONALLY DENSE FOODS ON THE PLANET. I'LL NEVER GET OVER THAT.

MAKES: 1¼ CUPS (345 G)

1 cup (237 mL) basic mylk (page 160)
1 tbsp (9 g) raisins
3 tbsp (27 g) chia seeds
½ tsp vanilla powder
½ tsp cinnamon

Blend everything but the chia seeds until smooth, stir in the seeds and wait a few minutes for them to gel. Enjoy! I like this served with fresh mint and cacao nibs.

CHEEZY GARLIC KALE CHIPS

I BET YOU CAN'T EAT JUST ONE.

MAKES: 4 CUPS (230 G)

2–3 bunches kale
1 cup (111 g) cashews
2 tbsp (19 g) nutritional yeast
Juice from 1 lemon
1 tbsp (17 g) miso paste
1 red bell pepper
1 tomato
1 garlic clove

Take the stems off the kale, then tear the leaves into large pieces (ideally the size of your palm); set aside the leaves in a large bowl. Blend the rest of the ingredients until smooth and the consistency of thick sauce. Work the sauce into the kale leaves with your hands, massaging the leaves as you go until every one is coated. Throw in the oven at its lowest temperature, or your dehydrator, for 2–3 hours or until the kale leaves become crunchy. Personally, I like them best before they get crunchy, so I suggest you taste-test at all stages!

RESOURCES

Read this chapter first! It has all the info you want and need that will help you learn your way around the kitchen as well as a new, healthier lifestyle! I've got a section that focuses on equipment, where I recommend what brands of juicers, blenders and food processors are best suited to you. I have a section on techniques, in which I explain some tips and tricks for easy juicing, blending and wholesome eating. I have a section that elaborates on some of the less common (but super awesome) ingredients I will be occasionally using in my recipes. Last, but certainly not least, I have created a section that includes lists of important books, documentaries and websites that have guided me on my own journey to long-term wellness, compassion and happiness. I think they might just change your life.

EQUIPMENT

Guess what? To make juice, you need a juicer. To make smoothies, you need a blender. Shocked? Yeah, I thought so (please note the sarcasm that those words were soaked in). If you don't want to spend a whack load of money, you don't have to be biting off your nails right now—there are very affordable options available. That being said, with increased price comes increased quality. The best juicers and blenders are an investment, but they are also well worth their cost. I suggest evaluating how serious of a juicer/smoothie drinker you are. How often do you drink or want to drink juice and smoothies? How often do you have time to? What is your budget? If you're just beginning your experimentation with this, start out with a less expensive piece of equipment and see if you are happy with it, or if eventually you want more. Tip: Before you buy a juicer, you can try using a blender to make juice. Blend up the ingredients for the juice recipe then strain them through cheesecloth or a sieve. Personally I think this should be used only as a temporary method because it's not as efficient; you lose a large amount of potential juice, but it works as a trial method. You can find all these pieces of equipment online (at Amazon.com, for example) very easily, or check out your local health food store and you might get lucky!

JUICERS

ENTRY-LEVEL: Hamilton Beach Big Mouth Juicer ($60.00).

MID-RANGE: Breville JE98XL ($145.00). I haven't used it myself, but a lot of people swear by it.

BEST: Omega VRT 350 ($370.00). It does it all, and it does it well. You can pump all kinds of fruits, veggies and greens into this baby every day and it never complains. Other excellent brands are Green Star and Champion.

BLENDERS

ENTRY-LEVEL: Hamilton Beach Wave Maker 10 Speed Blender ($60.00).

MID-RANGE: Ninja NJ600 Professional Blender ($100.00).

BEST: Vitamix 5200 ($400). It's the king of blenders (or queen, if we're into gender equality, and we are). Blendtec is on the same level, but I have my personal preference for Vitamix because it's all I've ever used, and I'd marry mine if I could.

FOOD PROCESSORS

You don't need one to make juice or smoothies, but in the Energy Bars & Healthy Snacks chapter (page 171) some recipes ask for a food processor. You can find them from anywhere between $50.00 to $200.00. I recommend Cuisinart or KitchenAid models. I use mine every single day to make everything from banana chocolate pudding to chili peanut sauce, so it's definitely a useful tool to have in the kitchen.

MYLK BAGS

If you haven't gotten to the chapter on mylks and mylkshakes yet, you're probably wondering what the heck I am talking about (and rightly so... a "mylk bag" sounds extremely strange and slightly freaky). Read page 160 first, then you'll dig me. These bags are used to squeeze out creamy mylk after you blend up nuts, seeds or coconut with water. You can alternatively use cheese cloth or a simple sieve, but I believe in using the right tool for the job... so spend $25.00 and get outfitted properly.

TECHNIQUES
JUICING

For quicker juice making, prepare your produce as soon as you buy it (if you know how often you make juice). Wash, peel and chop the produce as needed, then store in glassware in the fridge. If you have favorite juice recipes that you make frequently, put all the ingredients in one container, and make several containers (for example, make seven at the beginning of each week for speedy juice every day).

While using the juicer, alternate between juicing juicy fruits and harder vegetables and leafy greens (for example, switch between pieces of apple with kale leaves). This keeps everything lubricated and moving. Did that sound naughty? A little bit.

To get your juice ultra-smooth, I suggest straining it after it's been through your juicer. The machine will have already strained it to some degree but doing it a second time takes it to the next level. Yes, you will have next-level juice. This is a personal preference, though, and my mom actually likes her juice without any extra straining. To each their own.

If you are a busy beaver (or human) and don't have time to make juice every day or more than once each day—you can still have juice that often! Make it in batches that will last up to two days. I wish I could say make juice for a week in one day but honestly, it's only nutritionally worth drinking within 48 hours since it oxidizes very fast. Ideally you should be drinking your juice within 20 minutes but hey—life isn't fair, and we need to work with the schedules we each have. Store your juice in airtight glassware and keep in the fridge.

BLENDING

Like with juicing, if you know how often you will be making a particular smoothie recipe, prep your produce as soon as you bring it home and keep it in appropriate containers in the fridge.

To make really creamy, refreshingly cold smoothies, it's a good idea to have a fraction of the ingredients be frozen; frozen bananas or berries are my favorite to use, but any fruits or veggies will do…even dark leafy greens. I often add frozen kale or Swiss chard to my smoothies, and you can buy frozen spinach from most grocery stores. If frozen fruits or veggies aren't handy, just throw in a few ice cubes, but keep in mind this waters the smoothie down, so make sure to add a little less liquid, too.

This may seem obvious, but if your smoothie is too thick, add more liquid. If it's too thin, add more solids or superfood powders. I personally like mine pretty thin so I add 2–3 cups (473-710 mL) of liquid to my smoothies. If it tastes too watery, add a few dates or a tablespoon (7 g) of your fave superfood powder.

NOTE: I choose to buy mostly organic, so I prefer leaving the skin of my fruits and veggies intact (e.g., apples, cucumber, beets, carrots). When I buy non-organic produce, I peel most of it. We don't want pesticides in our juice! Ain't nobody got time for that. I understand that organic produce can cost much more than the conventionally grown stuff, but if you can afford it, choosing to support and eat organically grown food is very important. It will positively impact your long-term health, the well being of the planet and the local farmers who are doing honest work (not greedy mega-sized agribusiness corporations)!

INGREDIENTS

I sometimes use uncommon ingredients in my recipes. They're all incredibly powerful foods, but you may not have heard of them until now. Let's change that! I wanna give you a brief description of them, as well as explain why they're so darn good for ya. Many of these foods have been used to heal the body for thousands of years in cultures across the globe; they are the original tried-and-true players. You should be able to find the following ingredients in your local health food store or grocery store that has a selection of health food products. Alternatively, you can buy online (I recommend Upaya Naturals if you're in Canada).

• DATES: I think most folks have heard of dates, and you may even have tried them before. They're a dried fruit that comes from the date palm, originating around the Persian Gulf, and have been cultivated since forever ago (no, really—we've been eating dates for so long we can't even remember when we started). They are sweet, gooey, delicious bites of fudge in my opinion. I recommend using Medjool dates because they are the largest and have a unique caramel-like flavor, but any kind will work for my recipes. Always remember to take the pits out!

• CACAO: Cacao powder comes from the cacao bean and is an ancient superfood, originally consumed by the Mayan civilization to give them strength and mental focus. Basically, cacao is raw chocolate. It has amazing amounts of fiber, zinc and iron. It is also an aphrodisiac… *mmmhmmm*… If you can't find cacao powder, you can use cocoa powder instead.

- MACA: Maca powder is another superfood that comes from a root that grows in the mountains of Peru. It has hormone-balancing properties, and plenty of B vitamins and calcium. The flavor is pretty unique; it reminds me of molasses.

- SPIRULINA: This dark green powder is derived from algae and has impressive amounts of protein, essential amino acids and iron. You can tell by the deep, rich color that this food also provides a great dose of chlorophyll, which acts as a blood cleanser and takes part in many other essential functions.

- HEMP SEEDS: These little guys have a delicious nutty flavor and provide the perfect ratio of omega 3s and 6s, which work to improve brain function and play a role in metabolism. Hemp is an amazing food that can save the world! It's very energy-efficient to grow, and we can use it for everything from clothing to rope to paper...to food!

- FLAX SEEDS: Cultivated as early as 3000 BCE in Babylon, flax is a seed composed mostly of healthy fats— omega 3s—and fiber. It also provides great amounts of B vitamins, manganese and phytochemicals. Studies have shown it may help fight against heart disease, diabetes and cancer.

- COCONUT WATER: Coming from inside fresh young coconuts, coconut water is a super hydrating liquid filled with electrolytes and naturally filtered through the flesh of the coconut to give you pure refreshment. Buy your own coconuts and crack them open to get the water inside, or look for bottled 100% pure organic coconut water in the store.

- LUCUMA: This powder is derived from a fruit (coming from Andean valleys in Peru) and is popularly used to flavor ice cream because of its sweetly tart and fruity profile. It provides substantial amounts of carotene and several B vitamins.

- COCONUT NECTAR: I use this as a natural sweetener in a few of my recipes. Think of coconut nectar as a healthier maple syrup; it comes from coconut palms and undergoes minimal processing, which allows all the nutrients (including amino acids, B vitamins, vitamin C and minerals) to stay alive so you can benefit from them. If you can't find coconut nectar, you can use maple syrup instead.

- STEVIA: This white powder comes from the stevia plant and is one potent sweetener! It is calorie-free because the sweetness doesn't come from carbohydrates; instead it's simply the flavor of the plants' leaves. Use it very sparingly: only 1/16 of a teaspoon or less per single serving. You can also find stevia in liquid form, and in that case, just a few drops are needed.

- HIMALAYAN SALT: This is a mineral-rich salt that is mined in Pakistan, and I like to use it in very small amounts to enhance the flavor of some of my recipes. It's always optional if you prefer to keep recipes salt-free.

- COCONUT OIL: I only use virgin, cold-pressed, organic coconut oil, and I recommend you do the same if you wish to get all its wonderful health benefits. Coconut oil is composed of medium chain triglycerides that can have therapeutic effects on the brain because of how they are metabolized, as well increase your metabolism, which can lead to weight loss (if you need it)! Once digested, coconut oil has anti-bacterial, anti-fungal and anti-viral properties. I love using coconut oil on my skin as an all-natural moisturizer and sunscreen, too. If you are allergic to or can't find coconut oil, you can use cacao butter or cocoa butter instead.

BOOKS, DOCUMENTARIES & WEBSITES

These books, documentaries and websites have all helped me learn about healthy eating and living over the past few years. I think they will prove very useful to you as well. In my opinion, to succeed at anything (including long-term wellness) you need to be educated and informed about it.

BOOKS

- *The China Study* by T. Colin Campbell
- *Diet for a New America* by John Robbins
- *The Food Revolution* by John Robbins and Dean Ornish M.D.
- *Eat To Live* by Joel Fuhrman
- *Breaking the Food Seduction* by Neal D. Barnard
- *Raw and Beyond* by Victoria Boutenko, Elaina Love and Chad Sarno
- *Eating Animals* by Jonathan Safran Foer
- *Fast Food Nation* by Eric Schlosser
- *The Way We Eat* by Peter Singer
- *The Face On Your Plate* by Jeffrey Moussaieff Masson
- *Mad Cowboy* by Howard F. Lyman
- *The Thrive Diet* by Brendan Brazier
- *The Omnivore's Dilemma* by Michael Pollan
- *In Defense of Food* by Michael Pollan
- *Prevent and Reverse Heart Disease* by Caldwell Esselstyn
- *Becoming Vegetarian* by Brenda Davis and Vesanto Melina
- *Becoming Vegan* by Brenda Davis and Vesanto Melina
- *Becoming Raw* by Brenda Davis and Vesanto Melina

DOCUMENTARIES

- *Earthlings*
- *Making the Connection*
- *Queen of the Sun*
- *Forks Over Knives*
- *Zeitgeist* (series)
- *Food, Inc.*
- *The Corporation*
- *Flow*
- *Super Juice Me!*
- *King Corn*
- *Vegucated*
- *Fat, Sick & Nearly Dead*
- *Simply Raw: Reversing Diabetes in 30 Days*
- *Food Matters*
- *Hungry For Change*
- *The Future of Food*
- *Sweet Misery*
- *The 11th Hour*

WEBSITES

- Finding Vegan
- One Green Planet
- Renegade Health
- Natural News
- World Society for the Protection of Animals
- ForestEthics
- Happy Cow
- Vegan Body Building
- VegSource
- Fitness Blender
- Happy Healthy Vegan
- ADAPTT (Animals Deserve Absolute Protection Today and Tomorrow)

ACKNOWLEDGMENTS

Thanks to Page Street Publishing for asking me to write another book! I never wanna stop! Thank you Mum and Daddy, for your constant support, encouragement and confidence in me. You're my number one fan, Mom! Dan and Greg: I am grateful for your tolerance of my weird ways. To all my taste-testing friends, thanks for your seemingly bottomless stomachs and endless words of love. Hugs and kisses to every single person who has read and/or recommended my blog; you've brought me here and I'll never forget it! I'm on my knees in thanks (literally, I am sitting on the floor right now). Lastly and definitely not least, I have to thank you. Even if you don't know me, I can confidently say I think you're a beautiful, unique individual and I love you...for real.

ABOUT THE AUTHOR

EMILY VON EUW was born in and lives near Vancouver, British Columbia, Canada. She is currently—and casually—studying history, gender studies and philosophy at Simon Fraser University while she maintains her award-winning and popular food blog: This Rawsome Vegan Life. She is the author of *Rawsome Vegan Baking*: a cookbook all about raw, vegan, gluten-free desserts. When she's not drinking green juice or munching dark chocolate, she can be found passionately singing out of tune to Earth, Wind and Fire, whispering sweet nothings to flowers, watching Kubrick films, daydreaming about baby pigs, questioning the nature of reality and generally being excited about life...because life is way too awesome.

INDEX